· MEET ·
MARY CASSATT

Read With You Center for Excellence in STEAM Education

Read With You

Published by Read With You Publishing. Printed in the United States of America.
Read With You and associated logos are trademarks and/or registered trademarks of Read With You L.L.C.
ISBN:979-8-88618-092-3
First Edition January 2022

Afternoon Tea Party, 1890-1891

Young Mother Sewing, 1900

Little Girl in a Blue Armchair, 1878

Autumn, Portrait of Lydia Cassatt, 1880

The Boating Party, 1893-1894

Mother Playing with Child, c. 1897

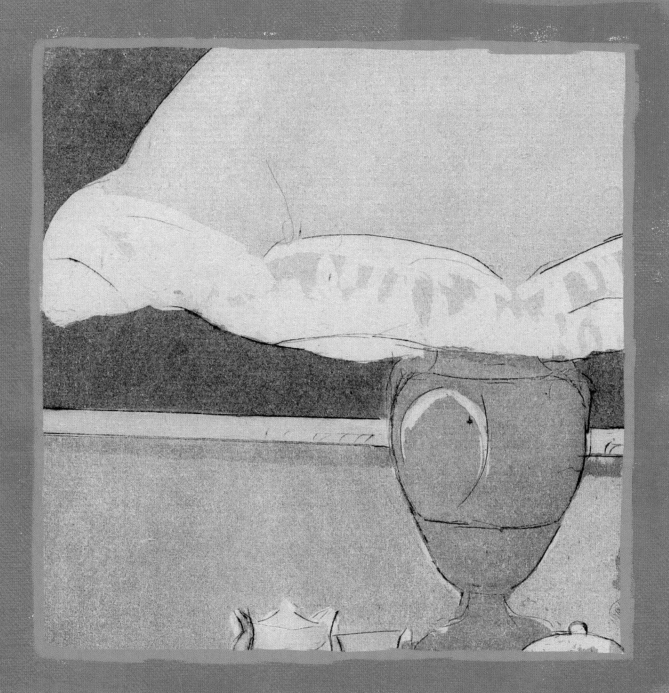

The Lamp, 1890-1891

Baby John with Forefinger in His Mouth, 1910

Find Examples

This painting is *Spanish Dancer Wearing a Lace Mantilla* (1873). Mary Cassatt was a part of the French Impressionist movement. They blended colors less, making the painting seem more like an idea than real life.

Do you think artists should paint women and children in their daily lives?

From the brushstrokes on the woman's clothing, you can see that this painting is not realistic. Do you like this painting more or less than a realistic painting?

Can you think of other famous paintings of women?

Connect

This painting is titled *Lydia Crocheting in the Garden at Marly* (1880). Lydia was Mary Cassatt's sister. Mary loved her sister very much and painted many beautiful paintings of her.

From this painting of Lydia and the one earlier in the book, what kind of person do you think Lydia was?

Who in your family would you like to paint a picture of?

If you painted them, what would they be doing in the painting?

Craft

Option 1

1. Choose a woman you respect or admire. Draw an outline of her in pencil doing something that she does every day.

2. Paint in the outline with watercolors.

Option 2

1. Find a bigger doll and a smaller doll. Pretend the big doll is the mother and the little doll is the child.

2. Place them on a nice chair or cushion. Try moving them around and see which position you like best.

3. Take a photo of your favorite position.

Made in the USA
Middletown, DE
01 September 2023

37793960R00022